THE ART OF MINDFULNESS

THE ART OF MINDFULNESS

A Guide to Inner Peace

B. VINCENT

QuantumQuill Press

CONTENTS

CHAPTER 1

Introduction

How do we get there? If this seems difficult to you, rest assured you are not alone. Decades of conditioning to believe that we are not enough, solely because we cannot be productive at every waking moment of our lives, take their toll. However, many of the world's most successful people practice stillness in some form, most commonly through meditation. Steve Jobs took long walks. Howard Stern has been a meditation devotee for years. Oprah Winfrey believes in "Remembering to breathe" with any mindfulness-based practice to help reduce your stress and live in the present. Ray Dalio "has said that meditation has been mindfulness and visualization," two things that are proven to deepen the experience, and as a result, you find the mind of a practitioner quick to adapt to the changing relationships between variables." What most people don't realize is that even the briefest periods of mindfulness can have positive effects. Not only will you enter a mindful state in just a few seconds, but it will also improve your integration with your business.

What does it mean to be mindful? In truth, the practice of mindfulness is unlike anything we've been taught to do by society. We live in a fast-paced, consuming world, a world that is almost afraid of stasis. Society tells us we must always be doing things, and we internalize that belief. However, there is a growing movement toward a world of quieter contemplation. Why now more than ever do so many people feel a need to change this? Because perhaps deep down, they are realizing the mistake of looking outside of oneself for true happiness. When we are in moments of chaos, often our first instinct is to run. However, perhaps escaping to the present is what we need to do instead of running away from the past and future.

CHAPTER 2

Benefits of Mindfulness

Practicing mindfulness can keep you grounded and humble, knowing that there are often tasks that we can't tackle alone. With practice, you may feel more a part of the world rather than apart. There are few other activities that can help calm and heal the body like relaxation and reflection. Looking deeper might even help find strengths and abilities that might have even been forgotten. Refocusing your vision and opening new doors to life and everything it has to offer. Looking in and on can help us tackle problems and inner conflicts that might be causing the blind spots that are standing in the way of success and growth in life.

Taking the time to relax and reflect can lead to a better sense of well-being. Relaxing and reflecting on life can also plant in our minds positive affirmations about ourselves, which can lead to a deeper respect for who we are. Being mindful of self and others and present in the moment can help lead to a deep sense of self and can help strengthen the relationships we have with others. Embarking on a quest for mindfulness can often lead the way to finding an inner peace that can help silence inner conflicts and battles. Silencing these battles can often help heal and calm the body, leaving you a stronger, more peaceful you. Strengthening this sense of self can also open the doors for happiness to enter.

2.1. Stress Reduction

The systems of mindfulness teach that by not becoming attached to any one thought and learning to breathe properly, people can become more effective managers of their stress response. By systematically beginning to avoid the body's external triggers and by satisfying the mind's internal demands, the body sends less energy to the amygdala, the body's intrusive worrying thoughts. With skill, intention, and practice, one becomes more able to detach from recurring self-criticism and excessive apprehension. It is well established that MBSR, as well as integrated-treatment programs, successfully alleviate numerous stress-related concerns and that people generally tend to be highly receptive to the teachings. At three months post-training, improvements to health and reductions in the swelling of the skin commonly seen with long-term stress were maintained. Trips to the doctor decreased 15-40% and participation in stress-related concerns remained abated for nearly all of the participants in the studies.

In situations where one feels outmatched, lacking in power, or overwhelmed, the stress response can be debilitating, particularly if it is not properly managed. When these moments are experienced in day-to-day life, they tend to accumulate and generate further responses culminating in chronic stress. Chronic stress can cause cerebral impairment, depression, immune deficiencies, neuroticism, debilitating anxiety, ulcers, heart disease, and diseases of the nervous system. The body can become so engrossed in managing chronic stress, that it literally exhausts itself. This can lead to death stemming from suicide, heart attacks, or other conditions that at the time of death may be indirectly related to stress such as high blood pressure or wellness. It's mindfulness and the decision to practice the teachings that can bring about real change to our lives with immediate and remarkable improvements to our health.

2.1. Stress reduction. Stress is a universal condition that affects everyone, in one way or another. Stress is not always a defeating force. In fact, in small amounts, it serves to motivate and quicken our thought processes. When opportunities and responsibilities are embraced, it energizes the body and mind for action. In this small measure, stress feels good. It is this stress response that drives the athlete to catch the discus or leaves the race car driver breathing heavily after he spends over three hours fighting for the winning position. Eustress is a term describing this kind of healthy and manageable induced stress. It is stress that is accompanied by excitement.

2.2. Improved Mental Clarity

Whether it is at work or at a personal level, we have all been so involved in what we were doing that we have lost time and space, and reacted quickly to something or someone, or answered something without thinking about it, then gradually regretted it. Later, once you start having more mindfulness in your daily life, it will soon happen that you reflect for a moment without reacting on the spot. You will start to notice that you do more reflex actions, that you drive faster, or that you do not eat properly. You may even notice that you act blindly, without really thinking or noticing what you do, for a short period of time at this moment. And knowing that, you will have the power to stop because instead of having an automatic reaction, you will be confronted with a moment of reflection.

Mindfulness and meditation help you regain mental clarity and focus, resulting in an increased feeling of stability and less internal opposition. Performing everyday tasks becomes easier because you approach them calmly and with a greater sense of control. If you find that your life is disjointed, mindfulness can be the tie that binds, giving you something to depend on as you analyze and dissect whatever seems to keep changing.

2.3. Enhanced Emotional Well-being

For most people, feelings of social isolation create a sense of negativity. Mindfulness techniques can help remove loneliness and bring a sense of belonging. A sense of positive interconnection results because your attention to the present moment allows you to remain conscious and be with the direct experience. Being mindful of social interaction can create a feeling of relatedness that can help reduce cynicism and mind-wandering and boost the overall quality of your conversations. Researchers have discovered that because of enhanced emotional regulation, individuals appear to be happier, more gratified, are less likely to experience depressive symptoms, and, overall, manage to control their emotions better.

Firstly, mindfulness fosters better control over your emotions, promotes a more positive disposition, and helps you to manage your emotions appropriately, particularly when somebody else's behavior triggers your negative emotions. This is often why mindfulness meditation is incorporated into therapy programs to deal with problems such as depression and anxiety. Furthermore, mindfulness can boost feelings of well-being, reduce levels of perceived stress, and enhance emotional resilience. As such, individuals become more capable of adapting to various challenges, especially those with stressful emotional consequences. In addition, practicing mindfulness techniques can result in a more optimistic disposition and reduced symptoms of depression and anxiety because of increased awareness of their thoughts and emotions, which leads to rational decision-making.

One of the most recognized benefits of mindfulness is the improvement in emotional well-being. Every human is susceptible to different emotions, whether good or bad. It is important to recognize your emotions and not let any of them control or overpower you.

The practice of mindfulness can help you become more emotionally stable and can induce feelings of comfort and relaxation. Many practitioners achieve significant improvements in various mental health conditions, including stress, anxiety, and depression.

CHAPTER 3

Techniques for Practicing Mindfulness

Visualization: Due to the power and activity of our minds without distanced thought, visualization has become a popular tool in sports, exercise, and even surgery. With our natural tendency to think vividly in images, aspects of our body physically respond in accordance with visualization, thereby improving performance. When we are able to experience images in as much detail as possible, our brains then make the minor distinction between a contained situation and reality. A vivid thought can have the same effect as a physical action. To this end, we can practice realistic firing sequences or creative alternatives, depending upon the situation.

Mindful breathing: This is a basic mindfulness meditation technique that you can use anywhere, at any time. It's a quick, simple way to be present for a moment. By following our breath through our body, we achieve a state of relaxation and focus throughout our daily routines. Through regular practice, we increase our ability to utilize the technique under stressful circumstances. Though inhaling is important, the most therapeutic component of the breath is the complete exhale, which engages the parasympathetic nervous system and shifts our focus away from the stress stimulus—thus, distanced thought.

Although mindfulness is easy to practice, it's difficult to incorporate it into daily life. As with any new habit, we find it tough to change the old, familiar habits. However, breaking out of our thoughts—distancing ourselves from them through techniques like meditation, visualization, and other strategies—allows for more freedom and creativity, better decision-making, and positive behavior shifts. Creating gaps between our thoughts is key to mindful breathing and has the ability to offer us a renewed and refreshed perspective. Here are a few suggestions for practicing mindfulness.

3.1. Breathing Exercises

I recommend a simple exercise that you can perform to teach your body to breathe effectively. One is placing both your hands over your abdomen, one on top of the other. This will supply you with information on when you're breathing in your chest as opposed to your abdomen. Breathe in and out, and you will notice that your chest expands instead of the abdomen. This is very good for becoming present, as it brings vitality immediately to your body. This will increase your awareness, recollection, and concentration, as well as lower levels of stress and anxiety. It will also release any accumulated emotional pain and blockage. To begin, let yourself go and allow the breath to flow. Do several abdominal breaths. 20 minutes of deep abdominal breathing will activate the vagus nerve, which releases mood-enhancing neurotransmitters like dopamine and serotonin. You'll still be able to continue with each day with peace of body and mind.

Breathing exercises. Take a seat in a straight-backed chair. Sit so that your back, neck, and head are aligned, but let your shoulders relax. You can close your eyes or leave them open and choose something small to gaze at without staring: the corner of a picture or a certain spot on the wall. Find that place and follow it with your gaze. That's how you should be and don't allow your eyes to wander. This may seem silly, and if it does, that's fine. But as you do it, allow yourself to see that piece you're focusing on as it actually is. It will help you calm your mind and focus. Let go of thoughts and allow your eyes to rest. And right there, connect with your breath. Start to pay attention to your breath. Is it in the abdomen? Most of us have shallow breathing that we clearly see in the chest. We want to calmly breathe from the abdomen, let the belly expand on the in-breath, and then exhale, breathing out completely. If you notice you're thinking of something else, gently bring your consciousness to your belly and continue with your breath.

3.2. Body Scan Meditation

This body scan meditation will change all of your following experiences, from showering, dressing, walking, and more because you focus on slowing down and enjoying the nuances of each moment. This moment-focused living will bring peace to your soul.

Begin at the top of your head and move your awareness slowly downward through your body, part by part. It's completely natural to become distracted, which is the best part of the body scan: instead of beating yourself up over losing your concentration, simply take a deep breath and guide your attention back to the place where you last felt relaxed. Remember, your judgment and frustration are just thoughts. Allow them to pass. Continue scanning through your body, part by part, until you have reached the bottoms of your feet. Take a few minutes to relax there. Then slowly bring your mind back to the room and surrounding sounds. You can slowly open your eyes.

The two most powerful times to use the body scan meditation are first thing in the morning and last thing before going to bed.

Here's an effective body scan that you can do today. Choose a time when you can practice without interruption. Find a comfortable place to sit or lie down. You can close your eyes or keep them open with a soft gaze in front of you.

3.3. Mindful Walking

When we walk, we are completely attentive to the sensations of walking. With each step, we are aware of the lifting of the foot, the bending of the various joints of the foot and leg, the movement of the various muscles, and the change in the muscles' tensions, etc. In this way, we experience many, many different feelings just in the simple activity of walking. As always with a mindfulness technique, the crucial element here is not the technique as such. The technique serves as the fulcrum from which to launch the journey into the inner self, a journey that has to be tailored to that individual to bring contentment – it is not the technique as such that is important, but the capacity to motivate the person to recognize that happiness can be found in the most simple of daily activities. Further, negative thinking ceases for a little while when we are intent on the exploration of our sensations. In addition, as with all the techniques, the act of training, of disciplining oneself, of persistently following a method, in itself instills a sense of accomplishment and satisfaction – high levels of happiness.

There are many forms of meditative walking. We may be stressed, lost in thought, and concerned with the many anxieties that afflict us modern humans; if so, this form of walking has nothing to do with mindfulness. On the other hand, walking can be a highly pleasurable form of moving about at a time when we are free from worries and are lost in admiring the beauty that surrounds us or in pleasant thoughts. However, this also is not mindfulness. Mindful walking is a technique used in mindfulness training. As one walks, one is fully aware of the sensations of walking. An uninstructed observer cannot see any difference between the walk of a mindful walker and that of another. However, the experience of the two is very different.

3.4. Loving-Kindness Meditation

May I feel safe. May I be happy. May I be healthy. May I have ease. Your mind empty and focus on each phrase. Together, and I come back to all four just try to think of one at a time. Then visualizing yourself and imagine feeling the emotions associated with each sentence. Really immerse yourself in each phrase or feeling. After you've said the phrases a few times, direct them towards someone you love, then say them and direct them to someone you're neutral about and then to someone you don't care for much, it's important to concentrate on the feelings of love, warmth and happiness.

If you've heard the term before but don't know exactly what it means, let me clarify. Loving-kindness meditation is a popular mindfulness technique that cultivates love and happiness for yourself and others. It's a simple practice: all you have to do is close your eyes, quiet your mind and repeat a series of positive affirmations. Like any new technique, it may be difficult at first, but with practice, it gets easier. Greater self-confidence, increased awareness and improved relationships with others after repeating the affirmations for four weeks have been argued to have such effects. Similar results were noted by other researchers. This ancient practice has been around for two and a half thousand years for good reason: it will improve your mindset and make you happier. Inspired? Make yourself comfortable, then try the following phrases for yourself:

CHAPTER 4

Integrating Mindfulness into Daily Life

Focus on tangible objects, but do not concentrate on them, except when it is strictly necessary for a particular purpose; instead, merely use them as the principal focal points for your attentive presence so that they can help you to remain aware of what is around you. As you walk down a street, look at the shop fronts, visit the fruit and vegetable market, and select the most appealing items; but all the while, incorporate large areas of all that is in sight within the embrace of your distributed existence. Be fully present, and allow the enchantment of watching absolutely everything to infuse itself into your actions. When talking to someone, ensure that you are there with the whole of your being; do not indicate assent or disagreement in a pre-programmed way, and do not fix your gaze on your interlocutor with the exclusive purpose of maintaining eye contact. If you do the latter, the intensity of the visual contact may become so strong that it keeps you confined within the narrow space of your eyes and the face of the other person.

During the day, you may find that the habit of being elsewhere is so strong that special means are required to remind you of your actual situation; otherwise, the continuity of presence which seemed so effortless in the morning becomes difficult as soon as you start performing the more exasperating duties of day-to-day living. Whenever you can, take frequent moments to feel your breathing, to become aware of the silent presence of all the normal activities in every cell of your body, and to perceive something of what is around you. This process need not be lengthy, conscious thought need not be involved; the simple sensation of the faithful emerging of each breath and of the symphonies silently orchestrated in the darkness of your physical container will increase your capacity for awareness. Then, during next actions, make full use of all your senses.

4.1. Mindful Eating

It may not seem challenging at all, but thoughtful eating is something that we lose quickly in a fast-food culture. Few people even take time to chew their food properly, which actually affects digestion. This new way of thinking about food also helps us to break free from emotional attachments to eating. For some of us, when we are sad, we begin feeling the need to binge eat or comfort ourselves with certain foods. When consuming nourishment with focus and deliberation, we are able to move away from this emotional dependency. Helping lose body image consciousness is a bonus as well. Avoiding negative feelings due to your relationship with food is key in our daily pursuit of inner peace, and is achievable with a simple redirection of thought. Enjoy the flavors, take your time to acknowledge feelings of hunger and fullness, and don't become sidetracked by anything else that competes for attention.

Mindful eating is a practice that reminds us to savor the luxuries in life - fresh, delicious food, and the people that we share it with. This is a concept that can be applied at any point in the day. When your mind is reeling with anxieties, bring it back by truly experiencing every bite of food that passes your lips. Pay attention to its taste, the way it feels against your tongue, and the way it smells. When practiced, this can be very spiritual and you may find that you have a more intense relationship with the food you eat after your experience.

4.2. Mindful Communication

We should be aware that we use jargon and try to find words that others understand, and we should be aware of what we say and what message we want to send. It is very important here to be aware of your feelings and thoughts. Before talking, always remember Aristotle's quotation: "It is the mark of an educated mind to be able to entertain a thought without accepting it." Communicate in that vein. Setting the goal for each conversation can also help. It doesn't matter how you'll do it, but it should be clear to you, and therefore to the other person. Be sure to notice when the conversation shifts away from that purpose. When necessary, gently return to this issue. Be mindful of your speech. Be mindful of your thoughts. Parenthood (and parenting) should be driven by awareness, so I encourage you to regularly practice mindfulness. Keep in mind that mindfulness will help you recognize and be at peace with painful situations.

"It depends on what the meaning of the word 'is' is." – President Bill Clinton, August 17, 1998, in Grand Jury testimony. We know that words have different meanings within different contexts. When dealing with the language of law, words take on a distinct meaning. Legal jargon is written in many if then and therefores, and sounds more like a dictation from a mathematical logic textbook than what most of us understand as communication. We use it to structure agreements, settle disputes or create penalties for violations, and in these aspects, communicate through law. Of course, there is communication aside from legal responsibility as well. We use communication in law informally, to understand others, listen to their worries and find solutions together. This communication requires a bit of talking and a lot of listening. A part of communication in law should also be about awareness.

4.3. Mindful Work

For many, the practice of mindfulness is difficult because it entails recognizing and dealing consciously with bodily sensations, emotional responses, and interpersonal communication patterns that might lead to frustration or anger. All these experiences in the workplace can start eating away at our sanity, and from here emerges the need for presence as well as the recognition that no event is in isolation or unrelated to our everyday activities. These practices can also help us to think twice during important or routine aspects of our work in general and leadership activities in particular. Mindful presence as an organizational leadership tool is very effective.

Practicing mindfulness at work means replenishing our mental and emotional resources so that in a short period of time, we can reach a state of balance and relaxation available for whatever challenges or opportunities may come. Looking after ourselves in the workplace does not necessarily mean improving by everyone at every task. However, the actual technique enables a focused, alert, and creative mind.

Technology has given us the choice of jobs to do and the places and hours to do them, and yet the constant overwhelm may leave people feeling disconnected and unproductive. In the workplace, it is possible to enhance well-being and also the working capabilities of an employee's sense of balance, appreciation, and focus. A century ago, Henry Ford introduced the eight-hour workday as a way of lessening the impact of personal and financial constraints on factory workers. While new technologies and communication forms allow us to connect to the professional and personal spheres of life, they also mean that on any given day, both aspects of our lives are demanding equal attention and are kept alive all the time.

4.4. Mindful Relationships

Relationships fail when one can't be present and actively connect with their partner. Failure to attend to the details of our most important relationships leads to hurt and trauma. Dr. Dan Siegel coined the term 'rupture/repair' to describe how repairing the hurt in a relationship can be the path to a stronger connection. Instead of pretending that hurt didn't happen, repair work lets both partners know that their needs are valid. This can be done by being divided when in a relationship. The art of mindful relationships is about presence in vulnerability and connection. It takes the little things for a relationship to thrive. When we actively share moments without seeking to fill them with empty chatter, we develop a trust that will protect us when the storms come. If you're having a bad day or things take a turn for the worse, this shared silence is something you revert back to like a security blanket.

The heart of mindfulness is being connected in the present moment. Mindfulness is a way to share space with others, friends, and even strangers. Rushing through our days and fighting to make deadlines, we often miss small opportunities to connect with others. The art of mindful relationships is all about being more present and connected to those around us. There is a feeling of fullness and joy that overcomes us when we walk through the world with an open heart, a sense of oneness, of being part of a larger whole. When we cultivate appreciation for the beauty and fragility of life, both around us and inside, we develop a more meaningful and satisfying connection to the world around us.

Milton Keynes UK
Ingram Content Group UK Ltd.
UKHW030908271124
451618UK00011B/331

9 798330 491995